Encountering God's Presence

Finding Strength in Adversity

MICHAEL NOWLIN JR

DEDICATION

To my beloved daughter Sarai,

You are the light of my life, the joy in my heart, and the inspiration behind so much of what I do. This book is dedicated to you, with all my love and gratitude for the endless ways you bring beauty and meaning into my world.

May the words within these pages serve as a testament to the depth of my love for you and the unwavering faith I have in the incredible person you are becoming. As you journey through life, may you always remember the strength, courage, and wisdom that reside within you.

With all my love,

“PaPa” Michael Nowlin Jr

Dear Reader,

Before you turn the pages of this book, I want to take a moment to express my deepest gratitude to you. Thank you for choosing to embark on this journey with me, for embracing the message of faith, hope, and redemption that these pages hold.

Writing this book has been a labor of love, fueled by a passion to share the timeless truths of God's Word with others. But it is your willingness to join me on this journey that brings these words to life.

As you prepare to delve into the depths of these pages, I want you to know that you are not alone. Whether you are facing trials and tribulations, seeking answers to life's toughest questions, or simply longing for a deeper connection with God, know that you are seen, you are heard, and you are loved.

May the words within these chapters serve as a source of inspiration, encouragement, and strength to you. May they remind you of the unshakeable hope we have in Christ and the boundless love He has for each and every one of us.

Thank you, dear reader, for your support, your encouragement, and your willingness to journey with me. May God richly bless you as you read, reflect, and grow in your faith.

With heartfelt gratitude,

Michael Nowlin Jr

ACKNOWLEDGMENTS

I would like to express my sincere gratitude to Nowlin Publishing for their unwavering support and belief in this project. Your dedication to excellence and commitment to bringing meaningful content to the world has been instrumental in shaping this book.

I am also deeply thankful to ABL Ministries for their encouragement and inspiration throughout the writing process. Your ministry's passion for spreading hope and light has been a guiding force behind the themes explored in these pages.

Additionally, I extend my heartfelt appreciation to CBDCF for their invaluable contributions to the research and development of this book. Your commitment to making a positive impact in communities worldwide has been truly inspiring.

Special thanks to ABL Publishing for their collaboration and assistance in bringing this book to fruition. Your expertise and professionalism have been indispensable in ensuring the quality and success of this project.

Finally, I am grateful to all the readers and supporters who have embraced this journey with open hearts. Your enthusiasm and encouragement have fueled my passion for sharing the message of hope with the world.

Together, may we continue to discover the harmony of hope in every aspect of our lives.

Warm regards,

Michael Nowlin Jr

Introduction

Embarking on a Journey of Faith

Welcome, dear reader, to the beginning of a journey—a journey of faith, hope, and redemption. In the pages that follow, we will embark on a quest to explore the depths of the human spirit and the boundless grace of God.

Life is a journey filled with twists and turns, peaks and valleys. Along the way, we encounter joys and sorrows, triumphs and trials. Yet, amidst the ebb and flow of life, there remains a constant—the unwavering presence of God.

In this book, we will delve into the timeless truths of Scripture, drawing inspiration from the Psalms, the Proverbs, and the teachings of Jesus and His disciples. Together, we will uncover the secrets of living a life of purpose, passion, and faith.

But more than just an intellectual pursuit, this journey is an invitation—a call to experience the fullness of life that God has promised to those who believe. It's a journey of discovery, as we unearth the treasures of God's Word and apply them to our daily lives.

As we embark on this journey together, I invite you to come with an open heart and a willing spirit. Leave behind the cares and concerns of the world and allow yourself to be immersed in the beauty and wonder of God's truth.

So, let us set out on this adventure, hand in hand, as fellow travelers on the road of faith. May this journey be a source of encouragement, inspiration, and transformation for us all. And may we emerge from its pages with a deeper understanding of who God is and who He has called us to be.

Chapter 1

Embracing Divine Guidance

In this chapter, we'll reflect on the significance of seeking and following God's guidance in our lives, drawing insights from Psalm 32:8 and Proverbs 3:5-6. As we journey through life, it's essential to trust in God's wisdom and direction, knowing that He alone can lead us on the right path.

Psalm 32:8 declares, "I will instruct you and teach you in the way you should go; I will counsel you with my loving eye on you" (NIV). This verse reminds us of God's promise to guide us and teach us His ways. Similarly, Proverbs 3:5-6 advises, "Trust in the Lord with all your heart and lean not on your own understanding; in all your ways submit to him, and he will make your paths straight" (NIV). These verses emphasize the importance of trusting in God completely and surrendering our plans to His perfect will.

When we seek God's guidance, we acknowledge our dependence on Him and our recognition of His sovereignty over our lives. It requires humility to admit that we don't have all the answers and to trust in God's wisdom above our own understanding. As we surrender our plans and desires to Him, He promises to direct our steps and lead us along the right path.

But why is it important to trust in God's guidance? Because He sees the bigger picture that we cannot. He knows the plans He has for us, plans for good and not for harm, plans to give us hope and a future (Jeremiah 29:11). When we trust in Him and follow His guidance, we can have confidence that He will lead us to the fulfillment of His purpose for our lives.

Moreover, seeking and following God's guidance brings peace and assurance amidst life's uncertainties. Even when the path ahead seems unclear, we can trust that God is leading us and that He will never leave us nor forsake us (Deuteronomy 31:6). His guidance is like a light shining in the darkness, illuminating the way forward and providing clarity and direction.

In conclusion, as we reflect on the significance of embracing divine guidance, may we trust in God's wisdom and direction as we navigate life's journey.

Let us lean not on our own understanding but acknowledge Him in all our ways, knowing that He will make our paths straight. So let us surrender our plans to Him and follow His guidance with faith and obedience, trusting that He will lead us to the fulfillment of His purpose for our lives.

Chapter 2

Finding Peace in Tough Times

Life can be pretty rough sometimes, right? It feels like we're always facing one challenge after another, and it's easy to feel overwhelmed and anxious. But guess what? There's a way to find peace even in the midst of all the chaos. Let's dive into some ancient wisdom found in the Bible that can help us out.

So, there's this part in the Bible, Psalm 46:1-3, that talks about how God is like our safe place when things get crazy. It's like saying, no matter what's going on—whether the world seems to be falling apart or everything feels shaky and scary—God's got our back. He's our rock, our fortress, our strength. Pretty reassuring, huh?

And then there's another part in Philippians 4:6-7 that tells us not to stress out about stuff but instead to talk to God about it. It's like saying, "Hey, when life throws curveballs at you, don't panic. Just pray about it, tell God what's on your mind, and thank Him for being there for you." And the cool thing is, when we do that, God gives us this crazy peace that we can't even explain. It's like having this super chill vibe even when everything around us is going nuts.

So, how can we make this stuff work in our everyday lives?

First off, we got to trust that God's got everything under control. He's like our superhero, always looking out for us, even when things seem totally out of whack.

Then, we need to talk to God regularly. Prayer is like texting your best friend when you need advice or just want to chat. It's a way to stay connected with God and find peace in the midst of all the craziness.

And don't forget about hanging out with other believers. They're like your cheerleaders, there to support you and remind you that you're not alone in this journey.

Oh, and here's a big one: try to focus on the good stuff, even when life gets tough. Being thankful for the little things can totally change your perspective and help you see that God is still at work, even in the midst of all the chaos.

Lastly, remember that true peace isn't about everything being perfect. It's about knowing that God is right there with you, no matter what. So, next time life throws you a curveball, just take a deep breath, say a little prayer, and trust that God's got this. You'll be amazed at how much peace you'll find in the midst of it all.

Chapter 3

Letting Go and Letting God

Ever heard the phrase "let go and let God"? It's all about surrendering to something bigger than ourselves and trusting that things will work out for the best. In this chapter, we're going to explore just how powerful it can be to surrender to God's will.

So, there's this verse in the Bible, Psalm 37:5, that tells us to commit our way to the Lord and trust in Him. It's like saying, "Hey, instead of trying to control everything and figure it all out on our own, let's hand it over to God and trust that He knows what's best for us." It's a pretty radical idea, but it's also incredibly freeing.

And then there's another verse in Romans 12:1-2 that talks about offering ourselves as living sacrifices to God. It's like saying, "Okay, God, here I am. Take me as I am and use me however you see fit." It's about letting go of our own desires and plans and surrendering to God's perfect will for our lives.

So, why is surrendering to God's will so powerful?

Well, for starters, it takes the pressure off of us. Instead of feeling like we have to have it all figured out, we can rest in the knowledge that God has a plan for us and that He's working everything out for our good.

Surrendering to God's will also allow us to experience true freedom. When we stop trying to control every little detail of our lives and instead trust in God's guidance, we're free to live without fear or anxiety. We can take risks, knowing that God is with us every step of the way.

And perhaps most importantly, surrendering to God's will helps us to align our lives with His purpose for us. Instead of chasing after our own ambitions and desires, we can focus on what God wants for our lives and how we can best serve Him and others.

So, if you're feeling overwhelmed or uncertain about the future, why not give surrendering to God's will a try? It might just be the most liberating and fulfilling decision you ever make.

Chapter 4

Embracing Thankfulness

Let's talk about gratitude. It's not just about saying "thank you" when someone holds the door open for you or gives you a gift. Gratitude is about cultivating a deep sense of appreciation for the blessings in our lives, big and small.

Psalm 100:4 tells us to enter God's gates with thanksgiving and His courts with praise. It's like saying, "Hey, when we come to God, let's come with hearts full of gratitude for all the good things He's done for us." And then there's 1 Thessalonians 5:18, which tells us to give thanks in all circumstances. That's a tough one, right? But it's also incredibly powerful. It's about finding something to be thankful for even when life gets tough.

So, why is cultivating a heart of gratitude so important?

Well, for starters, it shifts our perspective. Instead of focusing on what we don't have or what's going wrong in our lives, gratitude helps us to see the abundance of blessings that surround us. It's like putting on a pair of glasses that helps us to see the world in a whole new light.

Gratitude also has a profound impact on our mental and emotional well-being. Studies have shown that practicing gratitude can reduce stress, improve sleep, and increase overall happiness. When we take the time to acknowledge and appreciate the good things in our lives, it's like giving our brains a little boost of positivity.

But perhaps most importantly, cultivating a heart of gratitude strengthens our relationship with God. When we recognize and thank Him for the blessings He's given us, it deepens our faith and trust in Him. It's like saying, "Hey, God, I see what you're doing in my life, and I'm so grateful for it."

So, how can we cultivate a spirit of thankfulness in our lives?

Well, it starts with simply being aware of the good things around us. Take a moment each day to reflect on the blessings in your life, whether it's a beautiful sunset, a kind word from a friend, or a warm meal on the table. Then, take the time to express your gratitude to God for those blessings.

You can also make gratitude a regular practice in your life by keeping a gratitude journal or incorporating thankfulness into your daily prayers. And don't forget to express your gratitude to others as well. A simple "thank you" can go a long way in brightening someone's day and spreading a little bit of joy.

So, let's challenge ourselves to cultivate a heart of gratitude in all circumstances. Whether we're going through a rough patch, or everything seems to be going our way, there's always something to be thankful for. And when we approach life with a spirit of thankfulness, we'll find that our hearts are lighter, our minds are clearer, and our relationship with God is stronger than ever.

Chapter 5

Following God's Way

Let’s talk about obedience. It's not always the most popular topic, but it's so important when it comes to our relationship with God.

Psalm 119:1-2 tells us, "Blessed are those whose way is blameless, who walk in the law of the Lord! Blessed are those who keep his testimonies, who seek him with their whole heart." And then there's John 14:23, where Jesus says, "If anyone loves me, he will keep my word, and my Father will love him, and we will come to him and make our home with him."

So, what's the big deal about obedience?

Well, for one thing, obedience is a way of showing our love for God. When we follow His commands and live according to His word, it's like saying, "God, I trust you and I want to honor you with my life." And when we do that, it opens the door to a deeper intimacy with Him. It's like building a strong foundation for our relationship with God to grow and flourish.

Obedience also brings blessings. When we walk in obedience to God's commands, we position ourselves to receive His blessings in abundance. It's not about earning God's favor or trying to be perfect; it's about aligning our hearts with His and allowing His goodness to flow into our lives.

But let's be real, obedience isn't always easy. Sometimes, it means saying no to our own desires and surrendering our will to God's. It requires humility, trust, and a whole lot of faith. But the beautiful thing is that God doesn't leave us to figure it out on our own. He gives us His Holy Spirit to guide us and empower us to walk in obedience.

So, how can we walk in obedience to God's commands?

Well, it starts with knowing His word. The Bible is like our roadmap for life, showing us the way God wants us to live. Spend time reading and studying Scripture and ask God to help you understand and apply His word to your life.

Next, it's about surrendering your will to God's. Trust

that His plans are better than yours, and be willing to follow wherever He leads, even if it's not the path you would have chosen for yourself.

And finally, it's about walking in step with the Holy Spirit. When you feel that nudge to do something that aligns with God's word, don't ignore it. Listen and obey, knowing that God is leading you in the way that leads to life.

So, let's challenge ourselves to walk in obedience to God's commands. Let's seek to honor Him with our lives, knowing that as we do, we'll experience a deeper intimacy with Him and receive His blessings in abundance.

Chapter 6

Finding Joy in Salvation

Let's talk about joy. Not just any joy, but the kind of joy that comes from knowing we are saved by God's grace.

Psalm 51:12 says, "Restore to me the joy of your salvation, and uphold me with a willing spirit." And in Romans 15:13, it says, "May the God of hope fill you with all joy and peace in believing, so that by the power of the Holy Spirit you may abound in hope."

So, what's so joyful about salvation?

Well, first of all, salvation brings restoration. When we come to God in repentance and faith, He doesn't just forgive our sins; He restores us to a right relationship with Him. It's like being given a brand-new start, free from the guilt and shame of our past. That's something to be joyful about!

Salvation also brings renewal. It's not just a one-time

event; it's an ongoing process of transformation. As we walk with God and allow His Spirit to work in our lives, we become more and more like Jesus. Our hearts are changed, our minds are renewed, and we begin to see the world through God's eyes. That's something to rejoice in!

And finally, salvation brings everlasting hope. No matter what we face in this life – trials, hardships, even death itself – we have the assurance of eternal life with God. That's the ultimate source of joy – knowing that no matter what happens, we are secure in God's love and His promise of salvation.

So, how can we experience the fullness of joy found in God's salvation?

Well, it starts with recognizing our need for salvation. We have to acknowledge our sinfulness and our need for a Savior. Then, we need to believe in Jesus – that He died for our sins and rose again, conquering sin and death once and for all.

Next, it's about receiving God's gift of salvation with gratitude and humility. We can't earn it or deserve it;

it's a free gift from God, given out of His great love for us.

And finally, it's about living in the reality of our salvation every day. It's about remembering who we are in Christ and allowing His joy to fill our hearts, even in the midst of life's challenges.

So, let's embrace the joy of salvation. Let's celebrate the restoration, renewal, and everlasting hope that we have in Jesus. And let's share that joy with others, so that they too may experience the fullness of life found in God's salvation.

Chapter 7

Embracing God's Presence

Let's talk about experiencing God's presence in our lives – something truly transformative and powerful.

In Psalm 16:11, it says, "You make known to me the path of life; in your presence there is fullness of joy; at your right hand are pleasures forevermore." And in Acts 3:19, it says, "Repent therefore, and turn back, that your sins may be blotted out, that times of refreshing may come from the presence of the Lord."

So, what does it mean to encounter God's presence?

Well, first of all, it means seeking intimate fellowship with God. It's about making time to be still and quiet before Him, allowing Him to speak to our hearts and minds. It's about opening ourselves up to His love, His wisdom, and His guidance.

Encountering God's presence also means repentance and turning back to Him. It's about acknowledging our sinfulness and our need for His forgiveness. When we come to God in humility and repentance, He doesn't just forgive our sins; He refreshes and renews us, filling us with His presence and His peace.

And finally, encountering God's presence means experiencing the fullness of joy and abundant life that He offers. In His presence, there is no fear, no anxiety, no despair – only joy, peace, and hope. When we abide in Him, we find true satisfaction and fulfillment, regardless of our circumstances.

So, how can we encounter God's presence in our lives?

Well, it starts with making time for Him – prioritizing prayer, worship, and reading His Word. It's about creating space in our lives for Him to speak to us and reveal Himself to us.

It also involves cultivating an attitude of humility and repentance – continually turning away from sin and turning toward God. When we come to Him with a repentant heart, He promises to forgive us and refresh us with His presence.

And finally, it's about living in awareness of God's presence throughout our day – inviting Him into every aspect of our lives and trusting Him to guide and sustain us.

So, let's embrace the transformative power of encountering God's presence. Let's seek intimate fellowship with Him, repenting of our sins and turning back to Him, and experiencing the fullness of joy and abundant life that He offers. In His presence, we find everything we need for life and godliness, and we can rest assured that He will never leave us nor forsake us.

Chapter 8

Renewing Your Spirit

Let's explore the idea of restoring your soul, something we all need from time to time.

In Psalm 23:3, it says, "He restores my soul. He leads me in paths of righteousness for his name's sake." And in Jeremiah 30:17, it says, "For I will restore health to you, and your wounds I will heal, declares the Lord."

So, what does it mean to have your soul restored?

Well, it's about finding renewal and healing in God's presence. It's about experiencing His love and His grace in such a way that it revitalizes your spirit and refreshes your soul. When God restores your soul, He brings healing to the broken places in your heart and brings hope to the weary places in your soul.

It's also about being led by God in paths of righteousness. When you allow God to guide your steps, He leads you in the ways that are right and good, bringing peace and fulfillment to your life. When you walk in obedience to Him, you experience the abundant life that He promises to those who follow Him.

So, how can you experience soul restoration in your own life?

Well, it starts with coming to God with honesty and vulnerability – laying your burdens, your hurts, and your fears at His feet. It's about surrendering control to Him and trusting Him to heal and restore you in His timing and His way.

It also involves spending time in His Word and in prayer – allowing His truth to penetrate your heart and His presence to fill you with peace and joy. When you immerse yourself in His Word and in prayer, you open yourself up to His transforming power, and He begins to work in you to bring about healing and restoration.

And finally, it's about walking in obedience to God's commands – allowing Him to lead you in paths of righteousness and trusting Him to guide your steps. When you obey God, you position yourself to experience the fullness of life that He offers, and you open yourself up to His blessings and His favor.

So, if you're feeling weary and broken today, take heart – God sees you, He loves you, and He promises to restore your soul. Take time to come to Him, to immerse yourself in His Word and in prayer, and to walk in obedience to Him. As you do, He will bring healing and renewal to your spirit, and He will lead you in paths of righteousness for His name's sake.

Chapter 9

The Power of Togetherness

Let's take a closer look at the incredible blessings that come from unity among believers.

In Psalm 133:1, it says, "Behold, how good and pleasant it is when brothers dwell in unity!" And in Ephesians 4:3, it says, "Make every effort to keep the unity of the Spirit through the bond of peace."

So, why is unity among believers so important?

Well, when we come together in unity, there is a sense of harmony and peace that permeates our relationships and our communities. It's like a beautiful symphony where each instrument plays its part, creating a masterpiece of sound that is greater than the sum of its parts. When we are united, we reflect the love and the character of God to the world around us, and we become a powerful force for good in our communities and beyond.

In Ephesians 4:3, it talks about making every effort to keep the unity of the Spirit through the bond of peace. This tells us that unity is something that requires intentionality and effort on our part. It's not always easy to maintain unity, especially when we have different opinions or preferences, but it's worth the effort because where there is unity, God commands His blessing.

So, how can we pursue unity in the body of Christ?

First and foremost, it starts with humility and a willingness to put aside our own interests and preferences for the greater good of the body. It's about recognizing that we are all part of the same family – the family of God – and that we are called to love and support one another, even when we don't see eye to eye.

It also involves practicing grace and forgiveness – recognizing that we all make mistakes and that we all need grace. When we extend grace and forgiveness to one another, we create an atmosphere of love and acceptance where unity can flourish.

And finally, it's about focusing on what unites us rather than what divides us. We may have different backgrounds, cultures, and traditions, but at the end of the day, we are all united by our faith in Christ. When we keep our eyes fixed on Him and His love for us, everything else falls into place, and unity becomes a natural outpouring of our love for Him and for one another.

So, let's commit to pursuing unity in the body of Christ – to loving one another, supporting one another, and building each other up in faith. As we do, we can trust that God will pour out His blessings upon us, and that together, we can accomplish great things for His kingdom.

Chapter 10

Embracing the Call to Worship

Let's delve into why worship is so essential in the life of a believer.

In Psalm 95:1-2, it says, "Oh come, let us sing to the Lord; let us make a joyful noise to the rock of our salvation! Let us come into his presence with thanksgiving; let us make a joyful noise to him with songs of praise!" And in John 4:23-24, Jesus tells us, "But the hour is coming, and is now here, when the true worshipers will worship the Father in spirit and truth, for the Father is seeking such people to worship him. God is spirit, and those who worship him must worship in spirit and truth."

So, what does this tell us about worship?

First and foremost, it tells us that worship is not just something we do on Sundays when we gather together as a church – it's a way of life. It's about living every moment in the presence of God and recognizing His greatness and goodness in all things.

Worship is our response to God's love and grace, and it's a way for us to express our gratitude, praise, and adoration for who He is and all that He has done for us.

In John 4:23-24, Jesus talks about worshiping God in spirit and truth. This means that our worship should be genuine and heartfelt, coming from the depths of our souls. It's not about going through the motions or putting on a show – it's about being authentic and transparent before God, allowing Him to see us as we truly are and responding to Him with sincerity and reverence.

So, how can we embrace the call to worship in our daily lives?

First, it's about making worship a priority – setting aside time each day to spend with God in prayer, reading His Word, and praising Him for who He is and all that He has done. It's about cultivating a heart of gratitude and thanksgiving, even in the midst of life's challenges and struggles.

Second, it's about approaching worship with

reverence and awe – recognizing that we are coming into the presence of the Almighty God, the Creator of the universe. It's about humbling ourselves before Him and acknowledging His greatness and majesty.

And finally, it's about allowing our worship to flow out of a deep love for God – a love that is rooted in His love for us. When we truly understand and appreciate the depth of God's love for us, our natural response is to worship Him with all that we are and all that we have.

So, let's embrace the call to worship in our daily lives – let's make worship a priority, approach it with reverence and awe, and allow it to flow out of a deep love for God. As we do, we will experience the fullness of joy and satisfaction that comes from living in His presence and worshiping Him in spirit and truth.

Chapter 11

Conquering Fear with Faith

Let's explore the powerful theme of conquering fear through faith.

In Psalm 56:3, it says, "When I am afraid, I put my trust in you." And in 2 Timothy 1:7, we read, "For God has not given us a spirit of fear, but of power and of love and of a sound mind."

These verses remind us that fear is a common human experience, but we don't have to be enslaved by it. Instead, we can choose to trust in God's power and love, knowing that He has equipped us with everything we need to overcome fear.

So, how can we overcome fear with faith?

First, it's about recognizing that fear is a natural human emotion, but it doesn't have to control us. When we feel afraid, we can choose to turn to God in prayer and place our trust in Him. We can remind ourselves of His promises and His faithfulness, knowing that He is with us always.

Second, it's about focusing on God's power rather than our own limitations. When we face fearful situations, we can draw strength from the knowledge that God is sovereign and that nothing is too difficult for Him. We can trust that He is able to overcome any obstacle or challenge that we may encounter.

And finally, it's about embracing God's love and allowing it to cast out all fear. When we truly understand and believe in God's love for us, fear loses its power over us. We can rest in the assurance that we are deeply loved and cherished by our Heavenly Father, and that nothing can separate us from His love.

So, let's choose to conquer fear with faith – let's trust in God's power and love, knowing that He has equipped us with everything we need to overcome fear. As we do, we will experience a newfound sense of freedom and peace, knowing that we are held securely in the palm of His hand.

Chapter 12

Living with Purpose

Let's take a moment to reflect on the profound significance of living with purpose and intentionality.

In Psalm 90:12, we are reminded to "Teach us to number our days, that we may gain a heart of wisdom." And in Ephesians 2:10, it says, "For we are God's handiwork, created in Christ Jesus to do good works, which God prepared in advance for us to do."

These verses remind us that our lives are precious and purposeful. Each day is a gift from God, and He has a specific plan and purpose for each one of us.

So, what does it mean to live with purpose?

First, it's about seeking God's guidance and direction in all that we do. When we surrender our lives to Him and seek His will above our own, He will guide us into the purpose He has for us.

Second, it's about using our gifts, talents, and abilities to serve others and advance God's kingdom. Each one of us is uniquely created with gifts and passions that God wants to use for His glory. When we use our gifts to bless others and make a difference in the world, we are living out our purpose.

And finally, it's about living with intentionality and making the most of every opportunity that God gives us. Whether it's in our relationships, our work, or our daily interactions, we can choose to live with purpose by seeking to honor God in all that we do.

So, let's encourage one another to discover and fulfill God's purpose for our lives. Let's seek His guidance, use our gifts to serve others, and live with intentionality each day. As we do, we will experience the deep satisfaction and fulfillment that comes from living a life aligned with God's purpose and plan.

Chapter 13

The Hope of Redemption

Let's journey into the profound theme of hope found in redemption.

In Psalm 130:7, we read, "O Israel, hope in the Lord! For with the Lord there is steadfast love, and with him is plentiful redemption." Similarly, Titus 2:13 speaks of our "blessed hope, the appearing of the glory of our great God and Savior Jesus Christ."

These verses remind us that our hope is anchored in God's unfailing love and the redemption that is available to us through Jesus Christ. No matter how far we may have strayed or how broken we may feel, there is always hope in Christ.

So, what does redemption mean for us?

First, it means forgiveness. No matter what mistakes we've made or how many times we've failed, God offers us forgiveness through Jesus Christ. His blood shed on the cross covers our sins and cleanses us of all unrighteousness.

Second, redemption means restoration. God doesn't just forgive our sins; He also restores us to a right relationship with Him. Through Christ, we are reconciled to God and given a new life filled with purpose and meaning.

And finally, redemption means hope for the future. In Christ, we have the assurance of eternal life and the hope of being with Him forever. No matter what trials or tribulations we may face in this life, we can have confidence knowing that our ultimate destiny is secure in Him.

So, let's hold fast to the hope of redemption that we have in Christ. Let's trust in His unfailing love, receive His forgiveness, and embrace the new life He offers us. As we do, we will experience the joy and peace that come from knowing that we are truly redeemed and beloved children of God.

Chapter 14

The Power of Intercession

Let's explore the profound impact of intercessory prayer in our lives.

Psalm 141:2 invites us to, "Let my prayer be counted as incense before you, and the lifting up of my hands as the evening sacrifice." Similarly, James 5:16 tells us that, "The prayer of a righteous person is powerful and effective."

These verses highlight the significance of intercession, where we lift up the needs of others before God. Intercessory prayer is a powerful tool that allows us to stand in the gap for those in need, bringing their concerns before the throne of grace.

So, why is intercessory prayer so powerful?

Firstly, it acknowledges our dependence on God. When we intercede for others, we recognize that we cannot solve every problem or meet every need on our own. Instead, we turn to God, trusting in His wisdom, power, and goodness to intervene on behalf of those we pray for.

Secondly, intercessory prayer reflects God's heart of compassion. Just as Jesus intercedes for us before the Father, we are called to intercede for one another out of love and concern. In doing so, we participate in God's redemptive work, bringing healing, comfort, and restoration to those in need.

And finally, intercessory prayer unleashes God's power and grace. James 5:16 assures us that the prayers of the righteous are not in vain; they are powerful and effective. As we lift up the needs of others in prayer, God moves mountains, changes hearts, and brings about His purposes in ways we cannot imagine.

Therefore, let's encourage one another to pray fervently for one another. Let's lift up the burdens, struggles, and joys of those around us, knowing that our prayers have the power to make a difference. As we intercede for others, may we experience the incredible privilege of partnering with God in His work of healing, redemption, and transformation.

Chapter 15
Standing Firm in Faith

Let's dive into the vital aspect of standing firm in our faith.

Psalm 27:13-14 reminds us to, "I remain confident of this: I will see the goodness of the Lord in the land of the living. Wait for the Lord; be strong and take heart and wait for the Lord." Similarly, 1 Corinthians 16:13 advises us to, "Be on your guard; stand firm in the faith; be courageous; be strong."

These verses underscore the importance of unwavering faith, especially in the face of challenges and uncertainties. So, why is standing firm in faith crucial?

Firstly, it demonstrates our trust in God's promises. When we stand firm in our faith, we declare our belief that God is faithful, and His word is true. Despite the trials and tribulations, we may encounter, we hold fast to the assurance that God is with us and will never leave us nor forsake us.

Secondly, standing firm in faith fosters spiritual maturity. Just as a tree with deep roots withstands storms, our faith grows stronger when it is tested and proven. By remaining steadfast in our beliefs, we develop resilience, perseverance, and a deeper intimacy with God.

And finally, standing firm in faith empowers us to impact the world around us. When others see our unwavering trust in God, even in the midst of adversity, it serves as a powerful testimony to His faithfulness and goodness. Our steadfastness becomes a beacon of hope and encouragement to those who are struggling, pointing them towards the source of our strength.

Therefore, let's encourage one another to stand firm in our faith, regardless of the challenges we may face. Let's hold fast to God's promises, knowing that He is faithful to fulfill His purposes in our lives. As we stand firm in faith, may we inspire others to do the same, and may our lives reflect the glory and goodness of our steadfast God.

Chapter 16
Embracing Forgiveness

In this chapter, we embark on a journey into the transformative power of forgiveness, guided by the wisdom of Matthew 6:14-15 and Colossians 3:13. Forgiveness, often portrayed as a virtue, holds within it the key to profound healing and liberation, not just for ourselves but also for those we forgive.

Matthew 6:14-15 reminds us of the reciprocal nature of forgiveness—how our forgiveness of others is intertwined with receiving forgiveness from God. It's a powerful reminder that as we extend forgiveness, we open ourselves to the floodgates of divine forgiveness, freeing us from the burden of resentment and bitterness.

Colossians 3:13 further illuminates this transformative process, urging us to bear with one another and forgive as the Lord forgave us. It's an invitation to emulate the boundless grace and mercy demonstrated by God, releasing others from the debts they owe us, just as we've been released from ours.

Embracing forgiveness is not merely an act of magnanimity; it's a profound act of self-liberation. When we forgive, we untether ourselves from the chains of anger, hurt, and pain, allowing healing to permeate our hearts and souls. Moreover, forgiveness opens the door to reconciliation, restoring broken relationships and fostering peace.

As readers journey through this chapter, they're invited to reflect on their own experiences of forgiveness—both extending and receiving it. They're encouraged to confront the barriers that may hinder their willingness to forgive and to explore the immense freedom that comes from letting go of past grievances.

Ultimately, this chapter serves as a beacon of hope, illuminating the transformative potential of forgiveness. It's a call to embrace forgiveness not as a sign of weakness but as a testament to the resilience of the human spirit and the boundless grace of God. Through forgiveness, we have a path to healing, reconciliation, and profound freedom—a path illuminated by the divine light of love and grace.

Chapter 17

Navigating Trials with Trust

In this chapter, we embark on a profound exploration of trust—specifically, trusting God amidst the trials and tribulations that inevitably punctuate our lives. Our journey is guided by the timeless wisdom encapsulated in Proverbs 3:5-6 and James 1:2-4, offering invaluable insights into navigating the storms of life with unwavering faith.

Proverbs 3:5-6 serves as a steadfast anchor amid the tempest of adversity, urging us to trust in the Lord with all our hearts and lean not on our own understanding. It's a poignant reminder that our finite comprehension pales in comparison to the boundless wisdom of God. By acknowledging His sovereignty and entrusting our paths to Him, we find solace and direction even in the darkest of times.

James 1:2-4 further illuminates this concept, exhorting us to consider it pure joy when we encounter various trials, for they produce steadfastness and maturity within us. It's a paradigm-shifting perspective—one that invites us to view trials not as insurmountable obstacles but as opportunities for growth and refinement. Through perseverance, our faith is strengthened, and we emerge from adversity with a deeper understanding of God's faithfulness.

As readers journey through this chapter, they're invited to reflect on their own experiences of trials and difficulties. They're encouraged to embrace these challenges as catalysts for spiritual growth, trusting in God's providence and sovereignty. By surrendering control and leaning on His wisdom, they discover a profound peace that transcends circumstance—a peace rooted in the unwavering assurance of God's presence and guidance.

Ultimately, this chapter serves as a beacon of hope amidst life's storms, illuminating the transformative power of trust. It's a call to anchor ourselves in the unshakeable truth of God's promises, knowing that He is sovereign over every trial and tribulation we face. Through unwavering trust, we navigate the turbulent waters of life with courage, resilience, and an unyielding confidence in the goodness of our Heavenly Father.

Chapter 18

Cultivating Patience in Waiting

In this chapter, we embark on a journey to explore the virtue of patience—particularly in the context of waiting upon God's timing. With insights gleaned from Psalm 37:7 and Galatians 6:9, we delve into the profound significance of cultivating patience and endurance amidst life's uncertainties, trusting unwaveringly in the perfect timing of our Heavenly Father.

Psalm 37:7 serves as a timeless reminder to "Be still before the Lord and wait patiently for him." In a world characterized by hustle and haste, this verse beckons us to pause, relinquish our anxieties, and trust in God's sovereign orchestration of events. It's a call to surrender our desires and agendas, embracing the serene assurance that God's timing is impeccable—far surpassing our finite comprehension.

Galatians 6:9 further reinforces this message, urging us not to grow weary in doing good, for in due season we will reap a harvest if we do not give up. It's a poignant reminder that perseverance in the face of adversity yields abundant fruit—a truth that resonates deeply in the hearts of those navigating seasons of waiting and uncertainty.

As readers journey through this chapter, they're invited to introspect on their own experiences of waiting and longing. They're challenged to embrace patience as a transformative virtue—one that refines character, deepens faith, and fosters a profound intimacy with God. By relinquishing control and entrusting their desires to Him, they discover a peace that transcends circumstance—a peace rooted in the unwavering assurance of God's providence.

Ultimately, this chapter serves as a beacon of hope amidst the trials of waiting, illuminating the transformative power of patience. It's a call to surrender our timelines and agendas to the One who holds all things in His hands, trusting wholeheartedly in His faithfulness and goodness. Through patient endurance, we find strength, resilience, and an unshakable confidence in the divine orchestration of our lives.

Chapter 19

Living a Life of Generosity

In this chapter, we delve into the profound significance of living a life characterized by generosity—a virtue that transcends mere material giving and encompasses the entirety of our attitudes, actions, and intentions. Drawing wisdom from Proverbs 11:25 and 2 Corinthians 9:7, we embark on a journey to explore the transformative power of generosity and its profound impact on both the giver and the receiver.

Proverbs 11:25 imparts timeless wisdom, declaring that "A generous person will prosper; whoever refreshes others will be refreshed." This verse underscores the reciprocal nature of generosity, illustrating how acts of kindness and selflessness have the power to enrich not only the lives of others but also the life of the giver. It serves as a poignant reminder that true abundance is found not in hoarding wealth or possessions but in freely sharing what we have with those in need.

Similarly, 2 Corinthians 9:7 exhorts us to give

generously, not reluctantly or under compulsion, for God loves a cheerful giver. This verse emphasizes the attitude of the heart behind our giving, highlighting the importance of generosity that springs forth from a place of joy, gratitude, and love. It challenges us to reevaluate our motives and intentions, encouraging us to give freely and cheerfully, trusting in God's abundant provision and blessings.

As readers journey through this chapter, they're invited to reflect on their own attitudes toward generosity and examine the ways in which they can cultivate a lifestyle of giving in their everyday lives. Whether through financial contributions, acts of service, or simple gestures of kindness, they're challenged to embrace the joy of generosity and its transformative impact on both their own lives and the lives of those around them.

Ultimately, this chapter serves as a compelling call to action—a call to live lives marked by radical generosity and selfless love. It's an invitation to embrace the abundant blessings that flow from a heart willing to give freely and abundantly, trusting in God's provision and experiencing the unparalleled joy of making a difference in the lives of others.

Chapter 20

Pursuing Holiness in a Fallen World

In this chapter, we embark on a profound exploration of the call to pursue holiness in a world marred by sin and temptation—a world where moral relativism often blurs the lines between right and wrong, and where the pursuit of personal gratification often takes precedence over the pursuit of godliness. Drawing insights from 1 Peter 1:15-16 and Hebrews 12:14, we delve into the timeless wisdom of Scripture to uncover the transformative power of holiness and its profound significance in the life of every believer.

1 Peter 1:15-16 issues a solemn call to holiness, declaring, "But just as he who called you is holy, so be holy in all you do; for it is written: 'Be holy, because I am holy.'" These verses underscore the divine mandate for believers to reflect the character of God in every aspect of their lives—to embody holiness not as a mere external facade but as a genuine expression of their identity as children of the Highest. It challenges us to reevaluate our priorities and pursuits, urging us to align our lives with the standards of holiness set forth by our Creator.

Similarly, Hebrews 12:14 exhorts us to "make every effort to live in peace with everyone and to be holy; without holiness, no one will see the Lord." This verse emphasizes the inseparable link between holiness and our ability to experience intimate communion with God. It reminds us that holiness is not merely an abstract concept or a lofty ideal but a practical reality to be pursued diligently and earnestly. It challenges us to cultivate a lifestyle marked by purity, righteousness, and obedience to God's Word, knowing that it is through holiness that we draw nearer to the heart of our Heavenly Father.

As readers journey through this chapter, they're invited to reflect on their own pursuit of holiness and examine the areas of their lives where compromise and complacency may have taken root. They're challenged to confront the cultural pressures and societal norms that seek to dilute the call to holiness and instead embrace the radical countercultural mandate to "be holy, because [God is] holy." It's a call to strive for excellence in every sphere of life, knowing that true fulfillment and satisfaction are found not in conformity to the world but in conformity to the image of Christ.

Ultimately, this chapter serves as a powerful

reminder of the transformative power of holiness and its profound significance in the life of every believer. It's an invitation to embrace the call to holiness wholeheartedly—to pursue righteousness, godliness, and purity in a fallen world, knowing that it is through holiness that we experience the fullness of life and the joy of intimate communion with our Heavenly Father.

Chapter 21

The Gift of Discernment

In this chapter, we explore the invaluable gift of discernment and its critical role in navigating the complexities of life, drawing insights from Hebrews 5:14 and 1 Corinthians 2:14-15. Discernment empowers believers to distinguish between truth and deception, wisdom and folly, righteousness and unrighteousness, enabling them to make sound decisions and avoid spiritual pitfalls.

Hebrews 5:14 reminds us that "solid food is for the mature, who by constant use have trained themselves to distinguish good from evil." This verse underscores the importance of spiritual maturity and the cultivation of discernment through consistent engagement with God's Word and prayer. It challenges us to develop a discerning spirit that is attuned to the leadership of the Holy Spirit, enabling us to perceive the subtle nuances of spiritual realities and make wise, godly choices.

Similarly, 1 Corinthians 2:14-15 teaches us that "The person without the Spirit does not accept the things that come from the Spirit of God but considers them foolishness and cannot understand them because they are discerned only through the Spirit. The person with the Spirit makes judgments about all things, but such a person is not subject to merely human judgments." These verses highlight the indispensable role of the Holy Spirit in illuminating spiritual truths and guiding believers into all truth. They remind us that true discernment is not merely a product of human reasoning or intellect but is a supernatural gift imparted by the Spirit of God to those who walk in communion with Him.

As readers journey through this chapter, they're invited to cultivate a deeper sensitivity to the promptings of the Holy Spirit and to sharpen their discernment through prayer, meditation on Scripture, and fellowship with other believers. They're challenged to guard their hearts and minds against the subtle schemes of the enemy and to test every spirit against the standard of God's Word.

Ultimately, this chapter serves as a timely reminder of the importance of discernment in the life of every believer and the critical role it plays in safeguarding against deception and spiritual compromise. It's an invitation to embrace the gift of discernment as a precious resource for navigating the complexities of life and remaining steadfast in the truth of God's Word.

Chapter 22

The Journey of Spiritual Renewal

In this chapter, we embark on a transformative journey of spiritual renewal, drawing inspiration from Isaiah 40:31 and Romans 12:2. Spiritual renewal is a process of ongoing transformation whereby believers are conformed more and more to the image of Christ, experiencing a deepening intimacy with God and a heightened awareness of His presence and power in their lives.

Isaiah 40:31 declares, "but those who hope in the Lord will renew their strength. They will soar on wings like eagles; they will run and not grow weary; they will walk and not faint." This verse speaks to the promise of spiritual renewal for those who place their trust and hope in the Lord. It reminds us that God is the source of our strength and vitality, and as we wait upon Him in faith, He renews us inwardly, empowering us to overcome obstacles and endure hardships with unwavering perseverance.

Similarly, Romans 12:2 exhorts believers to "not conform to the pattern of this world but be transformed by the renewing of your mind. Then you will be able to test and approve what God's will is—his good, pleasing and perfect will." This verse underscores the transformative power of spiritual renewal, which begins with a renewed mindset—a mindset that is aligned with the truth of God's Word and liberated from the influence of worldly thinking and values. It challenges us to surrender our hearts and minds to the renewing work of the Holy Spirit, allowing Him to transform us from the inside out and conform us to the image of Christ.

As readers journey through this chapter, they're invited to embrace the process of spiritual renewal as a lifelong pursuit—an ongoing journey of growth and transformation in which they cooperate with the Holy Spirit's work in their lives. They're encouraged to cultivate spiritual disciplines such as prayer, meditation on Scripture, worship, and fellowship with other believers, recognizing their vital role in nurturing spiritual renewal.

Ultimately, this chapter serves as a beacon of hope and encouragement for those who long to experience the transformative power of spiritual renewal in their lives. It's an invitation to surrender to the renewing work of the Holy Spirit and to embark on a journey of deeper intimacy with God, knowing that in His presence, there is fullness of joy and everlasting renewal.

Chapter 23

The Courage to Stand Firm

In this chapter, we delve into the theme of courage and its indispensable role in the life of every believer, drawing inspiration from Joshua 1:9 and 1 Corinthians 16:13. Courage is the quality of spirit that enables believers to stand firm in the face of adversity, to persevere in the midst of trials, and to boldly proclaim the truth of God's Word in a world that often opposes it.

Joshua 1:9 declares, "Have I not commanded you? Be strong and courageous. Do not be afraid; do not be discouraged, for the Lord your God will be with you wherever you go." These words, spoken by God to Joshua as he prepared to lead the Israelites into the Promised Land, serve as a powerful reminder of the source of true courage—faith in God's presence and promise. They challenge us to overcome fear and discouragement with unwavering trust in God's faithfulness, knowing that He goes before us and fights on our behalf.

Similarly, 1 Corinthians 16:13 exhorts believers to "be

on your guard; stand firm in the faith; be courageous; be strong." This verse underscores the call to spiritual vigilance and steadfastness, urging believers to stand firm in the face of opposition and to courageously defend the truth of God's Word. It reminds us that true courage is not the absence of fear but the willingness to act in spite of fear—to remain resolute in our commitment to Christ and His kingdom, regardless of the cost.

As readers journey through this chapter, they're invited to examine their own lives and consider areas where they may be tempted to compromise or shrink back in the face of opposition. They're challenged to cultivate a spirit of courage—a courage that is rooted in faith, fortified by prayer, and emboldened by the indwelling presence of the Holy Spirit. They're encouraged to draw strength from the examples of courage found throughout Scripture and to emulate the faithfulness of those who have gone before us.

Ultimately, this chapter serves as a rallying cry for believers to embrace the call to courage—to stand firm in the face of opposition, to persevere in the midst of trials, and to boldly proclaim the truth of God's Word to a world in desperate need of hope and redemption.

Chapter 24

The Gift of Community

In this chapter, we explore the profound significance of community in the life of every believer, drawing insights from Ecclesiastes 4:9-12 and Acts 2:42-47. Community is a gift from God—a sacred fellowship of believers who support, encourage, and sharpen one another in their walk of faith.

Ecclesiastes 4:9-12 beautifully illustrates the power of community, declaring, "Two are better than one, because they have a good return for their labor: If either of them falls down, one can help the other up. But pity anyone who falls and has no one to help them up.

Also, if two lie down together, they will keep warm. But how can one keep warm alone? Though one may be overpowered, two can defend themselves. A cord of three strands is not quickly broken." These verses highlight the strength and resilience that comes from walking in community—a community where believers support and uplift one another, bearing each other's burdens and celebrating each other's victories.

Similarly, Acts 2:42-47 provides a vivid picture of the early Christian community, describing how believers devoted themselves to the apostles' teaching, to fellowship, to the breaking of bread, and to prayer. It speaks to the unity and generosity that characterized the early church—a community where believers shared everything they had, cared for one another's needs, and worshiped together with glad and sincere hearts. It challenges us to emulate the spirit of unity and mutual support found in the early church, fostering authentic relationships and deepening our sense of belonging within the body of Christ.

As readers journey through this chapter, they're invited to reflect on the importance of community in their own lives and to consider how they can actively cultivate and nurture meaningful relationships within the body of Christ. They're challenged to move beyond superficial interactions and to engage in authentic, Christ-centered fellowship—a fellowship marked by love, grace, and mutual accountability. They're encouraged to recognize the unique gifts and talents that each member brings to the body and to actively seek out opportunities to serve and edify one another in love.

Ultimately, this chapter serves as a celebration of the gift of community and a call to embrace the richness and depth of fellowship within the body of Christ. It's an invitation to walk alongside one another in love and unity, sharing in each other's joys and sorrows, and spurring one another on toward greater faithfulness and devotion to Christ.

Chapter 25

The Promise of Eternal Hope

In this final chapter, we turn our gaze to the promise of eternal hope—a hope that transcends the trials and tribulations of this present age and anchors our souls in the unshakable promises of God, drawing inspiration from Romans 15:13 and Revelation 21:4. Eternal hope is the confident assurance that God's purposes will ultimately prevail, and that He will bring to completion the work He has begun in us.

Romans 15:13 declares, "May the God of hope fill you with all joy and peace as you trust in him, so that you may overflow with hope by the power of the Holy Spirit." These words serve as a powerful benediction, invoking the blessings of joy, peace, and hope upon believers who place their trust in the God of hope. They remind us that our hope is not rooted in wishful thinking or human optimism but in the unchanging character and faithfulness of God, who is able to do immeasurably more than all we ask or imagine.

Similarly, Revelation 21:4 paints a vivid picture of the eternal hope that awaits believers in the age to come, declaring, "He will wipe every tear from their eyes. There will be no more death or mourning or crying or pain, for the old order of things has passed away." These words offer a glimpse of the glorious future that awaits God's people—a future where suffering and sorrow will be no more, and where we will dwell in the presence of our Heavenly Father for all eternity. They remind us that our present trials and tribulations are but temporary, and that they are working for us an eternal weight of glory beyond all comparison.

As readers journey through this final chapter, they're invited to fix their eyes on the promise of eternal hope and to anchor their souls in the unshakable promises of God. They're challenged to cultivate a deep and abiding trust in God's faithfulness, knowing that He who has promised is faithful to fulfill His word. They're encouraged to persevere in hope, knowing that their labor in the Lord is not in vain, and that a glorious inheritance awaits them in the age to come.

Ultimately, this chapter serves as a triumphant declaration of the promise of eternal hope—a hope that serves as an anchor for the soul, firm and secure. It's an invitation to embrace the hope that is set before us, knowing that it is our sure and steadfast anchor in the midst of life's storms.

Chapter 26

The Transformative Power of Love

In this chapter, we explore the profound impact of love in the life of a believer, drawing insights from 1 Corinthians 13:4-7 and 1 John 4:7-12. Love is the essence of the Christian faith, the defining characteristic of God Himself, and the greatest commandment given to believers.

1 Corinthians 13:4-7 provides a comprehensive definition of love, describing its attributes and actions. It declares, "Love is patient, love is kind. It does not envy, it does not boast, it is not proud. It does not dishonor others, it is not self-seeking, it is not easily angered, it keeps no record of wrongs. Love does not delight in evil but rejoices with the truth. It always protects, always trusts, always hopes, always perseveres." These verses challenge believers to embody the selfless, sacrificial love that Christ demonstrated in His life, death, and resurrection—a love that transcends human understanding and transforms lives.

Similarly, 1 John 4:7-12 emphasizes the inseparable

connection between love and God's nature, declaring, "Dear friends, let us love one another, for love comes from God. Everyone who loves has been born of God and knows God. Whoever does not love does not know God, because God is love. This is how God showed his love among us: He sent his one and only Son into the world that we might live through him. This is love: not that we loved God, but that he loved us and sent his Son as an atoning sacrifice for our sins. Dear friends, since God so loved us, we also ought to love one another. No one has ever seen God; but if we love one another, God lives in us and his love is made complete in us." These verses underscore the transformative power of God's love in the lives of believers and challenge us to reflect His love to others through our words, actions, and attitudes.

As readers journey through this chapter, they are invited to reflect on the depth and breadth of God's love for them and to consider how they can more fully embody that love in their relationships with others. They are challenged to love sacrificially, unconditionally, and extravagantly, knowing that love has the power to heal wounds, mend brokenness, and transform lives. They are encouraged to cultivate a heart of compassion, empathy, and forgiveness, allowing God's love to flow through them and touch the lives of those around them.

Ultimately, this chapter serves as a powerful reminder of the transformative power of love—a love that has the capacity to change hearts, restore relationships, and bring healing to a broken world. It is an invitation to embrace the profound truth that God is love, and to allow His love to permeate every aspect of our lives, shaping us into vessels of His grace and mercy.

Chapter 27

The Pathway to Humility

In this chapter, we explore the pathway to humility and its profound implications for the Christian life, drawing insights from Philippians 2:3-8 and James 4:6-10. Humility is the hallmark of true discipleship—a posture of heart that recognizes our utter dependence on God and acknowledges His supremacy in all things.

Philippians 2:3-8 provides a powerful example of humility in the life of Christ, declaring, "Do nothing out of selfish ambition or vain conceit. Rather, in humility value others above yourselves, not looking to your own interests but each of you to the interests of the others. In your relationships with one another, have the same mindset as Christ Jesus: Who, being in very nature God, did not consider equality with God something to be used to his own advantage; rather, he made himself nothing by taking the very nature of a servant, being made in human likeness. And being found in appearance as a man, he humbled himself by becoming obedient to death—even death on a cross!" These verses challenge believers to emulate the humility of Christ in their attitudes and actions, prioritizing the needs of others above their own and willingly embracing a posture of servanthood and sacrifice.

Similarly, James 4:6-10 underscores the transformative power of humility in the life of a believer, declaring, "But he gives us more grace. That is why Scripture says: 'God opposes the proud but shows favor to the humble.' Submit yourselves, then, to God. Resist the devil, and he will flee from you. Come near to God and he will come near to you. Wash your hands, you sinners, and purify your hearts, you double-minded. Grieve, mourn and wail. Change your laughter to mourning and your joy to gloom. Humble yourselves before the Lord, and he will lift you up." These verses highlight the close connection between humility and spiritual intimacy, challenging believers to humble themselves before God and experience His grace, mercy, and favor in their lives.

As readers journey through this chapter, they are invited to reflect on their own attitudes and motivations and to consider how they can cultivate a spirit of humility in their daily lives. They are challenged to surrender their pride, self-sufficiency, and self-interest to God, allowing His Spirit to transform their hearts and minds and conform them to the image of Christ. They are encouraged to embrace humility as a pathway to deeper intimacy with God, knowing that it is through humility that we experience His presence, power, and provision in our lives.

Ultimately, this chapter serves as a timely reminder of the transformative power of humility and its profound implications for the Christian life. It is an invitation to embrace humility as a defining characteristic of discipleship and to walk humbly before God and others, knowing that He opposes the proud but shows favor to the humble.

Chapter 28

The Gift of Contentment

In this chapter, we explore the transformative power of contentment and its profound implications for the Christian life, drawing insights from Philippians 4:11-13 and Hebrews 13:5-6. Contentment is the state of being satisfied and at peace with what we have, regardless of our circumstances or external conditions.

Philippians 4:11-13 provides a powerful example of contentment in the life of the apostle Paul, declaring, "I am not saying this because I am in need, for I have learned to be content whatever the circumstances. I know what it is to be in need, and I know what it is to have plenty. I have learned the secret of being content in any and every situation, whether well fed or hungry, whether living in plenty or in want. I can do all this through him who gives me strength." These verses challenge believers to cultivate a spirit of contentment in their lives, trusting in God's provision and sufficiency rather than relying on material possessions or external circumstances for their happiness and fulfillment.

Similarly, Hebrews 13:5-6 underscores the promise of God's presence and provision as the source of true contentment, declaring, "Keep your lives free from the love of money and be content with what you have, because God has said, 'Never will I leave you; never will I forsake you.' So, we say with confidence, 'The Lord is my helper; I will not be afraid. What can mere mortals do to me?'" These verses remind believers that true contentment is found in knowing and experiencing God's presence and provision in their lives, rather than in the accumulation of

wealth, possessions, or status.

As readers journey through this chapter, they are invited to reflect on their own attitudes and perspectives and to consider how they can cultivate a spirit of contentment in their daily lives. They are challenged to surrender their desires for material wealth, recognition, or success to God and to find their satisfaction and fulfillment in Him alone. They are encouraged to embrace contentment as a gift from God, knowing that it is through contentment that we experience true peace, joy, and fulfillment in life.

Ultimately, this chapter serves as a timely reminder of the transformative power of contentment and its profound implications for the Christian life. It is an invitation to embrace contentment as a defining characteristic of discipleship and to trust in God's provision and sufficiency in every season and circumstance of life.

Chapter 29
The Practice of Discernment

In this chapter, we explore the practice of discernment and its profound implications for the Christian life, drawing insights from Proverbs 3:5-6 and 1 Thessalonians 5:21-22. Discernment is the ability to distinguish between truth and error, wisdom and folly, righteousness and unrighteousness, and to make decisions that are aligned with God's will and purposes.

Proverbs 3:5-6 provides a foundational principle for the practice of discernment, declaring, "Trust in the Lord with all your heart and lean not on your own understanding; in all your ways submit to him, and he will make your paths straight." These verses challenge believers to rely on God's wisdom and guidance rather than their own human reasoning or intuition when making decisions, recognizing that His ways are higher than our ways and His thoughts higher than our thoughts.

Similarly, 1 Thessalonians 5:21-22 underscores the importance of discerning and testing everything in light of God's truth, declaring, "But test them all; hold on to what is good, reject every kind of evil." These verses remind believers that discernment is an ongoing process of evaluating and discerning the spirits, teachings, and influences that surround them, and holding fast to that which is true, honorable, and pleasing to God.

As readers journey through this chapter, they are invited to cultivate a spirit of discernment in their lives, relying on the Holy Spirit to guide them into all truth and wisdom. They are challenged to be vigilant and discerning in their thinking, attitudes, and actions, and to test everything against the standard of God's Word. They are encouraged to seek wisdom and counsel from godly mentors and spiritual leaders, allowing their discernment to be sharpened and refined through prayer, study, and fellowship with other believers.

Ultimately, this chapter serves as a timely reminder of the importance of discernment in the Christian life and its profound implications for spiritual growth and maturity. It is an invitation to embrace discernment as a vital aspect of discipleship and to rely on the Holy Spirit to lead, guide, and empower us to walk in wisdom and truth.

Chapter 30
The Pursuit of Holistic Health

In this final chapter, we turn our attention to the pursuit of holistic health—wholeness and wellness in every aspect of our being, drawing insights from Psalm 139:13-14 and 3 John 1:2. Holistic health encompasses the physical, emotional, mental, and spiritual dimensions of our lives, and reflects God's desire for us to experience abundant life and vitality in every area.

Psalm 139:13-14 celebrates the wonder and intricacy of God's creation, declaring, "For you created my inmost being you knit me together in my mother's womb. I praise you because I am fearfully and wonderfully made; your works are wonderful; I know that full well." These verses remind believers that they are fearfully and wonderfully made in the image of God, and that every aspect of their being is designed with purpose and intentionality by their Creator.

Similarly, 3 John 1:2 underscores God's desire for His people to experience holistic health and wellness, declaring, "Dear friend, I pray that you may enjoy good health and that all may go well with you, even as your soul is getting along well." These words express God's heart for His people to experience wholeness and wellness in every area of their lives, and His desire for them to prosper and thrive in body, soul, and spirit.

As readers journey through this chapter, they are invited to reflect on their own health and well-being and to consider how they can pursue holistic health in every aspect of their lives. They are challenged to prioritize self-care and stewardship of their bodies, minds, and emotions, recognizing that they are temples of the Holy Spirit and vessels of His grace and power. They are encouraged to seek balance and harmony in their lives, nurturing their physical, emotional, mental, and spiritual well-being through healthy habits, practices, and relationships.

Ultimately, this chapter serves as a reminder of God's desire for His people to experience abundant life and vitality in every area of their being. It is an invitation to embrace the pursuit of holistic health as an integral aspect of discipleship and to partner with the Holy Spirit in the journey toward wholeness and wellness in body, soul, and spirit.

Chapter 31
Pressing Onward in Faith

As we come to the close of this journey together, I want to take a moment to encourage you, dear reader. Throughout this book, we've explored the depths of faith, hope, and redemption, discovering timeless truths and profound insights that have the power to transform our lives.

But now, as you turn the final pages, I want to remind you that this journey doesn't end here. In fact, it's just the beginning. The lessons we've learned, the truths we've uncovered—they're not meant to be mere words on a page. They're meant to be lived out in the everyday moments of our lives.

So, as you close this book, I want to encourage you to press onward in faith. Whatever challenges you may face, whatever obstacles may come your way, remember that you are not alone. You have a God who loves you unconditionally, who walks beside you in every moment, and who has promised to never leave you nor forsake you.

Keep trusting, keep believing, keep pressing forward. And remember, the same God who brought you this far is faithful to carry you through whatever lies ahead. So don't lose heart, don't lose hope. Your story is still being written, and it's filled with promise, purpose, and possibility.

As you go from these pages into the pages of your own life, may you walk in the confidence of God's love, the assurance of His presence, and the hope of His promises. And may your journey be marked by faith, courage, and an unwavering trust in the One who holds your future in His hands.

Thank you for taking this journey with me. May God bless you richly as you continue to walk in His light and love.

www.ingramcontent.com/pod-product-compliance
Lightning Source LLC
LaVergne TN
LVHW010455160826
845677LV00012B/2501

* 9 7 9 8 8 8 2 1 8 3 2 6 3 *